BLACKBURN ROVERS

Sarah Blackmore

Published in association with The Basic Skills Agency

Hodder & Stoughton

A MEMBER OF THE HODDER HEADLINE GROUP

Acknowledgements

Cover: Nick Potts/Action Images.

Photos: pp. 14, 16 © Action-Plus; p. 22 © Allsport; p. 2 © Corbis; p. 6 © Newsquest (Lancashire) Ltd; p. 9 © PA News Photolibrary; pp. 20, 24 Sportsphoto Agency.

Orders: please contact Bookpoint Ltd, 39 Milton Park, Abingdon, Oxon OX14 4TD. Telephone: (44) 01235 400414, Fax: (44) 01235 400454. Lines are open from 9.00–6.00, Monday to Saturday, with a 24 hour message answering service. Email address: orders@bookpoint.co.uk

British Library Cataloguing in Publication Data
A catalogue record for this title is available from The British Library

ISBN 0 340 74739 0

First published 1999
Impression number   10 9 8 7 6 5 4 3 2 1
Year   2004 2003 2002 2001 2000 1999

Copyright © 1999 Sarah Blackmore

Typeset by Fakenham Photosetting Ltd, Fakenham, Norfolk.
Printed in Great Britain for Hodder & Stoughton Educational, a division of Hodder Headline Plc, 338 Euston Road, London NW1 3BH by Redwood Books, Trowbridge, Wiltshire.

Contents

1 The Dream

Blackburn Rovers have not always
been a dream team.
But they have always had a dream.

Jack Walker, a local businessman
who backs the club with money,
said in 1998,
'We will climb back to the top
and make this club a force.'

He was talking about Rovers in the Premiership.
He was talking about Rovers in Europe.

This has been Blackburn's dream.
They want to be top.
They work hard to be top.

It has not been easy.
It has not been cheap.

They have tried to make the dream come true.
They have been up and down.
It has been like a roller coaster ride.

The path to success can be like a roller coaster ride.

Let us board the roller coaster train.
The year is 1875.
This was the year that the club was formed.

The club had no ground.
All matches were played away.

Blackburn played their first home game in 1876.
They played at Oozehead Ground.
It was on Preston New Road.

One year later they moved again.
Rovers played at Pleasington Cricket Ground.
In 1878 they moved to Alexandra Meadows.

All this time the roller coaster was climbing.
Rovers moved to Leamington Road in 1881.
It was to be a lucky move.

2 Simply the Best

The Rovers' roller coaster reached the top.
In 1884, 1885 and 1886 they won the FA Cup.
Three years in a row!

Blackburn Rovers were simply the best.
They were given a special shield.
You can see it in the Boardroom today.

The roller coaster stayed at the top.
In 1890 they moved to Ewood Park.
And they did it again.
They won the FA Cup.

And just to show how good they were
they won the FA Cup again in 1891.

The roller coaster went higher.
Not only did they win the FA Cup.
They were winning the League as well.

Rovers were League Champions in 1912.
Then again in 1914.

But a roller coaster does not stay at the top.
It goes down.
It goes down fast.

Rovers won the FA Cup again in 1928.

3 Thrills and Spills

In 1928 the roller coaster was at the top.
Rovers were FA Cup winners again.
But hold on.
Down it goes . . .

1936.
Rovers went down to the Second Division.

Down it goes again . . .

1948.
Down to the Third Division.

The roller coaster was at rock bottom.
It had to climb up.
It was a slow climb.
It took ten years.
At last.
In 1950 Rovers were back in the First Division.

On with the ride.
In 1960 Rovers played Sheffield Wednesday
in the FA Cup semi-final.
What a match!
It was a real clash.

Blackburn won 2–1.
Derek Dougan scored the goals.
It was a brilliant game.
Harry Leyland played in goal.
He played the game of his life.

Derek Dougan scored the goals when Rovers
won the FA Cup semi-final in 1960.

Sadly the final was not so good.
The team lost to Wolves.

They also lost their full-back.
He broke his leg.
He had to be taken off.

Rovers lost at Wembley.
But played some great football.
The fans loved the players.
Some of the players became big stars.

The Rovers' roller coaster went up and up.
But it did not make it to the top.
Being champions of the First Division
was still a dream.

Down the roller coaster went in 1971.
Rovers went down to the Third Division.

The team climbed out of the Third Division
But went back down again in 1979.

The roller coaster climbed up again.
1981.
Rovers just missed going up to the First Division.
They lost on goal difference.

Hold on to your seats.
The roller coaster is going up.
This time it is a steep climb.

In 1987 Don Mackay came to Rovers.
He led the team to Wembley.
They beat Charlton Athletic.
They won the Full Members Cup.

Rovers tried.
They tried harder.
They tried again.
They were the first club
to have three play-offs in a row.
Play-offs to go up into the First Division.

In 1988 Rovers lost to Chelsea.
In 1989 they lost to Crystal Palace.
They were leading in the first leg.
But then lost.
In 1990 they lost to Chelsea again.

4 A Premier Dream Team

1991–1992.
Kenny Dalglish came to Rovers
as the new manager.
It was a thrilling season.

Rovers wanted to play with the best.
Their dream was to be the best.

They played Leicester City.
It was a tense match.
They played at Wembley, 25th May 1992.

They did it!
At last part of the dream had come true.
Rovers were in the Premier League.

Kenny Dalglish helped Blackburn Rovers
into the Premier League.

It was not cheap.
Blackburn played the transfer market.
Jack Walker backed them.
Kenny Dalglish bought players.

They spent more than 20 million pounds.
They broke a British record.
They spent 3 million pounds on Alan Shearer.

It paid off.
The roller coaster hit the top.
In the 1994–1995 season the dream came true.

Rovers spent 3 million pounds
on Alan Shearer.

Rovers were FA Carling Premiership Champions.

King Kenny and his team
scored the most goals in the league.
80 goals!

The Rovers' roller coaster was at the top.
There was only one way to go.
That was down.

It was the start of the 1996–1997 season.
Rovers' fans held their breath.

5 How Low Can Rovers Go?

Rovers got off to a bad start in 1996.
It got even worse.

Two big losses.
Right at the start of the season.

First to go was Shearer.
Then Dalglish left.
Results were not poor.
They were really bad.

Only four points from ten matches.
Not even a win.

How low can Rovers go?

Rovers v Newcastle.
September 1996.
Rovers had bad luck.

A penalty was turned down.
A Newcastle spot kick was given.
They were at the bottom.
Rock bottom in the Premiership.

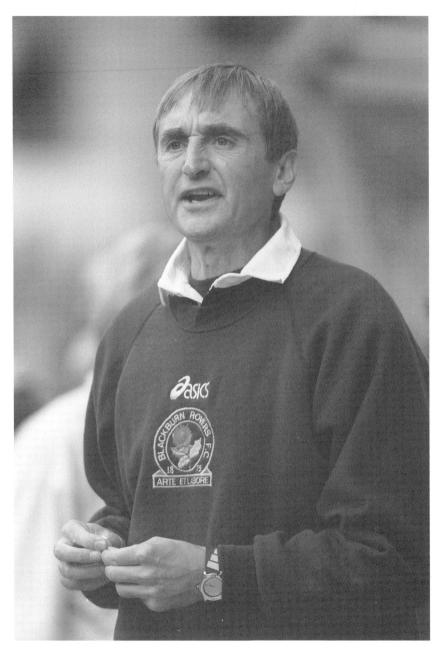

Tony Parkes.

6 On the Way Up

In October 1996 Tony Parkes
became caretaker manager.
He was to be there for the whole season.

Parkes' first home game was Rovers v Liverpool.

3rd November, 1996.
The date is in the mind of every fan.

A 3–0 win.
Chris Sutton put a penalty home.
Then he scored a second.
In the second half.

Chris Sutton put an end to a run
of bad luck.

Shearer came back in December.
He was wearing black and white stripes.
The colours of Newcastle.
Hendry and Berg made sure
he did not see the Ewood goal.

The climb had started again.
The Rovers' roller coaster was on its way back up.
Rovers got 11 points in five matches.

In December 1996, Shearer was playing for the other side.

Blackburn Rovers.
The Blue and White Army.
A Premier team, here to stay.

From now on, the only way is up.
And Rovers are looking to manager Brian Kidd
to take them there.

Kidd became Rovers' new boss in December 1998.
He came from his job as assistant manager
at Manchester United.
It will be Kidd's job to make sure
that the Rovers' roller coaster keeps going up.
Right into the millennium.

The fans and players think he is the man to do it.
'The new manager is going to be good for all of us –
me, the players and the fans,'
says Rovers' striker, Kevin Davies.

7 Goalscoring Record Breakers

Player	Record	Goals
Simon Garner	Most goals scored in Rovers' career	192
Ted Harper	Most goals scored in a season	44
Alan Shearer	Fastest 'ton' in club history	100 goals in 124 matches
Tommy Briggs	Most goals in one match (8–3 win over Bristol Rovers 1955)	7

If you have enjoyed reading this book, you may be interested in other titles in the *Livewire* series.

Sheffield Wednesday
Derby County
Leeds United
West Ham United
Arsenal
Newcastle United